# IN MY HEAD

## VOL. II

## J. M. STORM

*Monarch Publishing, 2018*
*www.monarchbookstore.com*
*Instagram: @monarchpubishing*

# CONTENTS

# 1

## JUST LIKE FADED LOVE

you have to hurt sometimes
before you can heal.
but be careful, sometimes
we become attached to our
pain.
it's personal and intimate
and completely ours.
that can be hard to let go
of, just like faded love.

i'm not lazy,
but i love lazy
days with you.
and i'm not afraid
to be alone,
but i am afraid to
be without you.

she loved him for
many reasons, but
she loved the way
he made her laugh.
because it's hard
to stay focused on
all that stresses
you when you erupt
into laughter.
it's childlike.
back when we weren't
so serious.
and every chance he
had, he would take
her back there.

some things are better
without giving any
thought.
no thinking, just doing.
we can walk the rope
until the moment we begin
to think of how we are
walking it.

someone who can admit
when they are wrong is
someone who has a great
appreciation for truth.

one day you will
fall and fall hard.
and you will smile
the entire descent.

i think you have to
get a little lost
for your feet to
understand the path
that feels like home.

you should always
give your best.
but always remember
not everything
deserves what you
have to give.

sometimes people don't
want the answers. they're
not ready for them just
yet. all they need is for
someone to understand where
they are. someone to feel
it so they don't feel so
alone in it.

you will always be a
part of me. you will
always speak to me
in the chaos and in
moments of quiet
like salt in the ocean,
you are part of me.

sometimes you learn
what you were made
for. you learn what
it is that you were
meant to do, but not
yet.
i felt that way when
i saw you.
that is the woman i
will love the rest
of my days.
not just yet, but soon.

sometimes people will
go in a direction you
never expected.
all you can do is love
them, even if it takes
them away. because that
is really the only
reason you'd want
someone to stay.

time changes
"it didn't work
out"
into
"it worked out,
just not like
i expected."

it may feel like it
is all over now.
like no matter how
hard you try, your
heart will never be
the same.
it probably won't.
we change and grow
throughout our lives
and the heart is no
exception.
sometimes a heart in
pieces is a heart
with room to grow.

that's the thing.
we think we need a lot,
and we do. but it isn't
the things we work so
hard for.
we need someone to love
us. to say they're proud
of us.
that no matter what, they
believe in us.
and the person we need to
hear that from the most
is ourselves.

i just want to be
with you. because
being away feels
a little too much
like being broken.
because even when
you're not holding
me, you're holding
me together.
just by being you,
just by being there.

you just feel right.
and that means
something from one
who has felt so much.

before you say,
i love you,
you should know
that it isn't
enough.
once it was, but
i've grown and
it no longer is.
i need respect.
i need space.
and i need
someone who
understands the
meaning of honor.

it's beautiful,
this thing between
her and i.
it's rare.
it's sacred
and it's so infinitely
indescribable.

and it's not for
public consumption.

one day you'll look back
and you'll realize you
had it all. even in the
times you thought you
had nothing.
because there are so
many things we just take
for granted that we
almost become immune
to them.
one of the biggest tragedies
in life is to only
know appreciation for
a few big things.

trying sometimes feels
a lot like failing.

keep trying.

you are the name
i whisper in my mind
whenever i want to
feel home.

she took care of the
things she needed to
for the future.
and if she never
found the one she
always hoped she'd
find, she would be
just fine.
but deep down she
would always be a
dandelion in the
desert. just wanting
to be someone's
only wish.

i want to take care
of you, knowing full
well that you can
take care of yourself.
that's what happens
when you fall heart
first into someone.
your heart becomes
bigger and capable
of so much more than
you ever knew.

i don't care
what everyone before
me wanted from you.
i just want to hear
the pages that you want
to read aloud, but fear
no one wants to hear.

i am still.
which is to say
i haven't moved
since i fell for
you.
i am still and
yet every bit of
me oscillates
to the frequency
of you and me.
like
honey bee wings,
we defy reasoning.

sometimes you have
to feel your way to
the answers.
because sometimes the
right and wrong of it
all isn't read or
spoken. it's not black
and white but endless
shades of gray that
good or bad, you have
to feel.

maybe one day we
will learn to lay
down our arms and
refuse to fight
the war inside
with the ghosts
of the past.
one day we climb
out of the trenches
and stand in no mans
land and raise our
glass to the things
that never happened.
to the things we
wish we could take
back.
to the person we
thought we knew.
the person we thought
we would be.

and everything i find
beautiful, holds a
piece of you.

the story goes like this;
people walk through life
and sooner or later
everyone falls.
many pick themselves back
up but some stay on the
ground because hope is
an exhaustible thing.
and once it's gone, it
hurts more than the fall.

Somewhere along the way,
I became ok with being
alone and the further I go
in this solitude, the more
resistant I am to leave
it behind. Not to say
there aren't times I don't
feel the whisper of loneliness
on my neck, because I do.
But I know it'll pass
and that alone doesn't
justify having someone,
at least not to me.
I've reached a place where
I'm not interested in
anything less than
absolutely fucking amazing.
Because anything less
than that and I'd rather
be alone.

# 2

## THE BEAUTIFUL SIDE OF MAYBE

she picked herself
up and she put
herself back together
and was last seen
on the beautiful
side of maybe.

we had a talk, just
like we did back then.
but it was different.
maybe it was to not
hurt the other or maybe it was
out of respect, but
we talked and we
danced around the
obvious.
connections rarely
die, they're
abandoned.

some will see the
beauty on the outside
of you and others will
judge it. grade it.
give it a number.

hold on to those who
see the beauty on
the inside of you.

i've heard all
the goodbyes
and i've swallowed
down the ones i
never got and i'm
past all that.
i'm at a place
where i just don't
care anymore,
except for that,
which is meant
to stay.

it is not about
finding the most
beautiful.
it is about finding
the one who makes
you see the beauty
outside your own
comfort zone.

she is beautiful.
but you really cannot
comprehend it until
you understand that
she is the result
of the pieces that
she refused to let
life take from her.

make her laugh often.
because one of the most
beautiful things is to
see her smile gone wild.

sometimes i wonder
if there are others
like me.
who feel everything
and everything has
a feeling.

some search everywhere
for a cure, something
to make them whole,
when all along it was
locked away inside.
because many times the
only thing that is
wrong with us, is our
view of ourselves.

one of the worst
feelings is to
feel last, by the
one you put first.
it is a feeling
your heart won't
ever accept.
no matter how
much you love
them, revolt is
inevitable.
just as it should be.

you've gotta slow down
and let yourself heal.
because open wounds
don't heal if they
never close.
slow down darlin.
not for me, but for
yourself because
only you can do this.
only you know where
the stitches belong.

that's the thing about
love. it's neither
rich or poor. it has no
grasp of the concept
of money.
it has no secrets, and
tells no lies.
and it demands nothing,
but instead looks to
what it can give.
love is never the
problem. it is our
interpretation of
what love is.

some will find
great pleasure
in provoking a
reaction from
you. that's
when you need
to discover
the great
pleasure in
giving them
none.

don't be the fool
who is more concerned
of how other men
look at your woman,
rather than how she
sees the look you
hold for her.

and if you ever feel
like you've missed
your chance at what
you've always wanted,
you must consider
the possibility that
what you've always
wanted is what you've
always known. and what
you need and what you
deserve is bigger than
you can imagine.
because sometimes missed
chances were never ours
to begin with.

she gets to me in
so many ways, but
one is how she is
a woman of grace
and class, and yet
she is not above
getting her hands
dirty.
because she is so
different from me.
her beauty and
femininity are like
an opiate.
but her willingness
to do what needs to
be done, always
feel like home.

i hope the life you
live is the life
you love. the life
you've always wanted.
but if it isn't,
take heart.
sometimes you don't
know what that is
until much later.
when you're ready
and when the look
of it all doesn't
matter so much.
all that matters
is how it feels.

i don't have an explanation
as to how you pull me in,
you just do.
you've always had a gravity
that i've never been able
to overcome.

sometimes i stay up
too late and i think
too much and once
again i feel you more
than i should.
but i've always had
a weakness for you,
even if it's just
your memory.

sometimes we're silent
because our soul knows
how it feels, but hasn't
found the words that
the mind can understand.

and i think it was
the feel of you that
told me you were it.
because i've felt many
things in my life,
and somehow, no matter
how great, i knew
i could live without
it. until i felt you.
there was something
inside of me that
couldn't let go.
not just the feel
of you, but the
feel i had of myself.

she loves her
independence,
and yet sometimes
she likes to be
told what to do.
that's part of her
contradiction and
part of her magic.
and part of your
magic will be when
you understand.

some will love your
outside and some
will fall in love
with your actions,
but they aren't
meant for you.
hold out for the one
who falls in love
with your inside,
the broken pieces
and all.
not because it is
wrapped by your
beautiful shell,
but because it feels
like home.

if they think they
can do better, then
let them go. let them
go find the answer to
their riddle.
everyone deserves
someone who looks at
them as a masterpiece
and wouldn't change
a thing.
and the truth is,
they've just shown
you that you can do
better.

on the way to
finding the
real you, you
must accept that
it might mean
the death of what
every one thought
you to be.
just as the
butterfly can no
longer be a
caterpillar.

one day you grow up.
you love not because
it works in your
favor, or because you
are tired of being
alone.
one day you understand
it perfectly. one day
you love because you
are unable to stop it.

and what many don't
realize is that the
things they can't
let go of are that
way because they
are held in the
heart and not the
hands.

i still feel you,
but it's what you
used to be. and that
is a far cry from
what you are now.
that's how it is
for everyone.
we're all changing,
every single day,
and when you stop
talking they
become two people.
who they were and
who they are.

she had such restraint
to turn away from what
she really wanted and
i think that's what
drew me in deeper.
i wanted to be her
weakness. her achilles
heel. the needle in
her arm.
i wanted to be the
wind that toppled her
walls. but in the process,
she became all that
to me.

# 3

# SOMETHING NEW CAN GROW

and if you feel
like life is
consuming you
in its fire,
remember this.
sometimes it is
necessary for the
land to be scorched
and its history
purified before
something new
can grow.

i didn't just fall in
love with you, i fell
in love with how you
saw the world.
and it was through
those eyes i saw what
i was missing.
i saw home.

i hope that when
you finally find
your way that you
still hold out your
hand to those who
are still searching.
because sometimes
that's all it takes
to change a life.
someone who knows
where they are going
and yet they pause.
they pause because
they remember and
they care.

i learned the meaning
of success not by
having more, which
once upon a time i
believed, but in the
realization of how
little I really needed.

you and me,
we speak
the same
soul language.

all i ask is
that you love
me with a madness
that scares you
sometimes.
because in that
moment it's
choosing between
what you feel
and what you fear.
and even though
it's normal to
feel fear, don't
ever fear what
you feel.

i'm not going
anywhere.
that's what
happens when a
heart is
touched as deep
you did mine.
new pretty things
have no feel and
that is their
downfall.
i am addicted
to your feel.

she's made it through
the dark and into the
light.
like a midnight wish,
made a thousand times,
that finally came true.

some things you just
know the answer to
long before you know
the question, and
that was true with you.
i knew i needed you
in my life in some way,
long before i knew why.

everyone has wings,
but not everyone
believes they
can fly.

she has good days
and some that
are bad.
some feel like
flying and others
feel too much
like dying.
and none of that
matters.
because every day,
she is doing the
best she can.

we place value on
the things that we
strive for, and that
is our mistake.
our time is where
the true value is.
you can't borrow
more of it, you
can't steal it and
you can't buy it
what you've got is
all you've got.
and once you
understand that,
you begin to recognize
what is worth your time.

i look at you
and i want to
build things.
four walls and
a roof.
a roaring fire.
a beautiful day
where the world
could never find
us.
that's what you
do. you make
these hands
ache for beautiful
work.

paint me out to
be whatever you wish
but just know that you
cannot escape the
colors from staining
your hands and it
will always speak
more about you
than it does of me.

deep down she made
him see that the
young girl still
lived somewhere
inside.
and part of her
magic is that she
also made him
realize that the
young boy he once
knew, also survived.

i know i'd be ok
without you, but
i wouldn't be me.
the me that i've
become just from
being close to you.
you bring a clarity.
a balance. i don't
just see it, but
i feel it.
you make me a
better me.

and if i could make
you understand one
truth, it would be
this.
someone who manipulates
your feelings through
guilt isn't loving you.
that's an attempt to
control you.
and that has nothing
to do with love.

the very best
i love you
doesn't come
from an
obligated mind,
but from a
grateful heart
that has grown
so much and yet,
still cannot
contain it.

some will say,
i love you,
because they
expect it back.
and some will
say the exact
same thing
because it is
their truth.

bad things will
happen and hard
times will come,
that you can be
certain.
but always
remember that it
is just a land
you're passing
through and not
your home.

so many memories
come to me in
black and white,
except yours.
your colors refuse
to be silent.

and you'll know
you're on your
path when it
really doesn't
matter what
anyone thinks
of it.
all that matters
is you're going
to the place
you've always
belonged.

be with someone who
understands the
value of just being
in your presence.
because time is all
we truly have, and
if anyone should
understand that basic
law, it should be
the one who says
they love you.

because everyone doesn't
hurt the same. it brings
out different demons in
each of us. it takes us
back to things we thought
we had put to rest.
some will take it and
give it back to the one
they love because the one
they love brought it out.
but that isn't love.
that's getting even.
that's anger.
that's jealousy.
that's a loss of control
of oneself and it is better
to walk away with love.
not just for them, but
for yourself.

letting go doesn't mean
forgetting. it means
realizing and accepting
it is not a part of
your reality.
letting go is letting
it become just a memory.

sometimes the most
beautiful things
wait for us, but we
must walk to them.
it is a walk of
faith. a test that
reveals how much
we believe it is
ours to have.

she is the whiskey
i drank in the bar
i never meant to go in
on the street i never
meant to walk down
and yet i find myself
never wanting to sober
up

i don't like to fight,
it's not in my nature.
but you must also
know if i am forced
into a corner,
survival is.

i believe love goes on,
even when all hope is
gone. if it ever was,
on some level, it will
always be. even when
you know they've burned
your fingertips too many
times to ever have
sensitivity to feel them
like you once did.

love is infinite.
but trust is exhaustible.

# 4

## PIECES OF THE UNIVERSE

i can be yours
or i can find
a new way.
because that is
what humans do.
they adapt. they
change. it is how
we survived.
but i am not all
human. i am made
of pieces of the
universe, and those
pieces have memory.
and that is why
i'll always want
to stay with you.

some of my
happiest places
are in my mind
with you.
i don't need to
see the world,
but i can't stop
myself from feeling
you.

sometimes
the first step to
getting it right
is to own the
possibility that
we had it all
wrong before.
that is what will
separate you from
so many.
because we live in
a world where there
is a certain shame
associated with
admitting being
wrong. everyone wants
to be right, if only
in their mind.

we all have a
breaking point.
but thankfully,
we are provided
with a turning
point as well.

if you believe
she is a flower,
then you must know
she needs sun and
rain.
she needs more than
just bright light
attention.
you have to sink
down to her roots
to appreciate
where her beauty
comes from.

i think we all wander
the darkness, chasing
the light that catches
our eyes, without
realizing until much
later, the brightest
light we know, burns
inside.

we all make deals
to go forward.
some make them with
others and some make
them with themselves.

the world might not
like what you have
to say.

but that's not why
you were given a voice.

i love it when
you reach for
my hand for no
other reason
than standing
next to me just
isn't close
enough.

she's not new to love
or heartache. but she
is brand new just the
same. because for the
first time she has no
plans. she's not trying
to figure it all out.
she is present in each
and every breath and
that's how it feels,
brand new.

she thinks that she
loves the things that
can break her.
but that is just an
illusion because she
doesn't know the
depth of her strength.
because nothing has
broken her yet.

i don't expect
every person to
get me.
because i find
pleasure in
both the simplest
of things and the
complexity of
thought.

people want to have
nice things. so they
work hard, sometimes
too hard. unaware
that the nicest things
are free, but can't
be owned. only experienced.

sometimes it won't
stay whole, no matter
how much you try to
hold it all together.
and that's when the
hard part comes.
when you have to let
go of it all and let
it be what it's
supposed to be.

once you've felt great
love, you won't forget
it. even though there
may come a day when you
want to because it hurts
to remember.
but you'll always remember.
that's the price of
extraordinary love.
it's unforgettable, even
when it has passed in
and out of existence.

in the end it comes
down to the
moments of beautiful
honesty with yourself.
moments that you didn't
give a damn what
everyone else thought.

your job isn't to please
so many others. it isn't
to be accepted by everyone.
your job is to find your
personal peace, and when
you find that, you'll
find true happiness.
that will piss off some
people.
understand that is the cost
of being you.
but also understand that
you are worth it.

i caught myself thinking
about you and what used
to be.
and i don't know why the
mind does that, going
back to places that it
can never really go back
to.
maybe it is to heal.
maybe it is to punish.
or maybe it is to just
understand how i got
here.

true love is hard
to come by because
it is two souls
who have found the
love in giving.
it's not about what
they receive.
it's about what they
can provide.
it's about what they
can put on their
own shoulders and
carry away.

you may not be ready,
and that is ok.
sometimes you have to
learn as you go.
but you do have to be
committed. because
that's how things
happen. that's how
things get done.
by deciding what you
want.

and the best poetry,
is the one i will
never write.
the story of her
and i.
and how it happened
and how fate sung
a song that only
we could hear.

we all lose our way
at some point and
sometimes that is
a good thing. In fact,
sometimes it's the
best thing.
because sometimes
it never was ours
to begin with.

pain.
it's so universal and
yet so intimately
personal.
i tell you i know
your pain, and on some
level, i do. and yet
i don't really know
it at all.
i only know my
version. that is to
say, i only know the
way my skin has been
cut. i only know the
nerve endings in my
own flesh, which isn't
the same.
but it is enough to
emphasize, enough
to feel.

stars are not born
without pressure.
remember that.
stay true.
stay intact,
and welcome the
metamorphosis.

we think we know ourselves,
but many of us don't.
i didn't, but i didn't know
it. that's the thing. the
catch 22. how could i not
know me?
you get so used to a routine,
day in and day out.
we are creatures of habit.
we ask all kinds of questions
in our life, but none are as
meaningful or as bold as
the questions we present to
ourselves. what makes me
happy, or sad and why
is that?
we all feel things and we
all have triggers.
it's how we respond.
it's the volumes.
ask those questions and
follow the answers and
you'll know the secrets
to the universe.
at least the part that
pertains to you.

she has a warrior spirit
inside and if you want
to get close to her,
closer than anyone has
before, then embrace the
fighter.
don't be intimated by
it, that's not what it's
about. we all fight
battles, mostly alone
and unknown.
and all we really want
is someone to look at
us with love and to say,
without saying a word,
"it's ok to lay down
your arms."

we have our own
language,
you and me.
one that doesn't
have a word for
goodbye.

# 5

## THE WORTH OF YOUR HEART

love is difficult
because so many
have it backwards.
they look as to
what love can
give them.
as long as their
list of needs are
met, they will
love in return.
but that's not the
way love works.
love always looks
for what it can
give more than
what it can get.

there has been times
that i had to learn
how to crawl again
before i could learn
how to stand up and
walk away.

i don't claim to
have all the answers,
but i do believe that
everytime you follow
fear, you end up a
little further away
from who you were
meant to be.

they're going to
try to get back
in, but you're
stronger than
that.
you know you are.
so show them.

everybody has a
reason for the
things they do.
they don't have to
believe in it or
maybe they aren't
even aware of it.
but the reasons
are always there.

we were good together,
once.
and maybe that was just
the beginning, where
you put your best foot
forward.
or maybe we wanted to
believe in a math that
would reconcile itself.
it doesn't really matter
except for the fact that
we believed, once.
and that always makes me
smile.

i saw your worth from
the very beginning.
but it was more than
that, gold is something
you use but don't feel.
and that is what had me.
the feel.
and the truth is that i
could never walk away
with the knowledge that
you love me.

sometimes it doesn't
work out like we
planned. like the story
isn't obeying our wishes.
but that's life.
we have our dreams and
plans and then there is the
way things turn out.
and somewhere in between
there is the small window
where we can adapt.
and that magic window is
where we change our lives.

i'll hold you until
it's all gone.
the pain, sadness, all
of it. all gone.
"but what if it never
completely goes away?"
she said

then i'll keep holding.

i don't know everything
and i never will. and
mostly, i am ok with
that.
as long as i know the
feel of sliding down
the straps of your
dress and the waterfall
in your kiss.
as long as i know your
taste and have heard the
sound of your submission
in your sighs, then i
know all that matters.

you are the water
and i am the salt
and what we have
together is bigger
than anything else
on earth.

she remembers the words
as if they were said
yesterday.
and in some small way,
that's what happened.
part of her got stuck
in that place where
time stands still.

i just want it all.
i want to hold you
together and yet at
the same time,
completely unravel
you.

home.
it's different things
for different people.
but for us, it's
where the walls come
down and the clothes
come off.
the bed isn't made
but our love is.
it's the place where
we laugh and love
and sometimes cry.
it's the place where
our souls are free.

i often don't remember
my dreams, but i
always know when i've
dreamed about you.
i wake up facedown
on your side of the bed.
and as crazy as it sounds,
i can feel you. not
physically, but i feel
your presence and i
just know that you were
here. even if it was
just a dream.

there's times that
we make love and it's
beautiful.
but then there's times
that i need you raw.
and needing.
and all the pretenses
have gone out the
window.
you tell me to fuck
you.
it's not asking, it's
telling.
and as your man i see
you in a beautiful
light. a light that
washes over me.
cleansing any doubt
that i may have had.
you're beautiful.
unashamed and unapologetic
about what you want
from me.

i always wanted you.
even when i didn't
know what i wanted.
even before i knew
you.
it was you.
you were the chapter
that i didn't know
the words to, but
always knew it existed.
and when i finally
found it and began
to read, i knew i
was home.

maybe i stayed too long
because i wanted to
believe that it could
eventually work.
or maybe i stayed purely
for the comfort a
known quantity brings.
even if it's bad, you
know how bad.
what ever the case, what
kept me hanging on wasn't
working anymore.
and when you've reached
that point, you've reached
the end.
sometimes we wait
for the end.
and sometimes
the end waits
for us.

all i want to do
is be next to you
and follow that
path until the end.
over the mountains
and through the
gorges,
your path is mine.

i wanted you and i
was ready for the
deluge.
i wandered too many
deserts and remembered
too many things.
i was ready to tear
off my shirt and bathe
in your downpour.
forgetting everything
before.

sometimes love becomes
a person and is no
longer an independent
thing.
they are one in the
same.

he cared for her in
his heart, long before
he did with his hand.
just as he undressed
her with his words
long before his touch.

maybe you just
don't get it.
i fucking care
about you.
and maybe that
doesn't sound
like much, but
i've learned to
be cautious in
what i care
about.

one day it will all make
sense.
one day you will realize
that those who couldn't
or wouldn't stay are just
a reminder of what you at
one time thought you wanted,
before you learned the
worth of your heart.

claim her publicly
and unequivocally
claim her privately

i love the simple
moments of no choice
like carrying you to
bed and feeling your
arms and legs wrapped
around me.
simple moments of no
going back, no turning
around.
moments that we have
no choice but to
consume.

that's the thing, you
can't go back. there
is only moving forward.
moving from this moment
onto the next.
to carry anger,
jealousy and hatred is
to prolong it.
leave it in the moment
and keep walking.

looking back, i had always
felt out of place.
not to say that i didn't
belong, but more that i
felt the pull
of another time and place.
i know now that is the feel
of being in transit.
not yet knowing you.
and yet, i was on my way
to you.

i know you've
been hurt and
i know the
bruises have
left your
heart tender.
i'm here, but
i won't push
you.
anything that
is worth having
is worth waiting
for.
and sometimes
you have to wait
for a beautiful
heart to heal.

i love the tension
that keeps building
between us. like a
rope that is being
stretched tighter
and tighter.
both of us beginning
to ache for the
moment it breaks.

i just have to be
close to you, one
way or another.
either physically,
emotionally or
mentally.
and sometimes i
need all of it
at once.

i want you to remember
one thing. wherever
you are and wherever
you may go, you will
always be loved. until
my last breath and
beyond, you will be
loved.

i stay busy but
inevitably I find
myself alone with
your words.
and I think that's why
there are some people
you never really get
over.
their words made their
way in and found a
home in your soul.

i think of who i
was and now who
i am and the thing
that separates those
two is you.

i've got it bad
for you.
and i know this
drink isn't the
answer.
but it numbs and
softens the sharp
edges of you
not being here.
and i keep thinking
that there will be
a bright day soon
where i'll walk in
the sun.
and i'll dry out
a bit and forget
that you belong
here.

take a chance.
because it is in the
chances we take when
we are most alive.
it is where we cheat death
in our living.

i like the way your
lips feel on my neck
and the way your breath
dances on my skin.
i like the way it feels
like it was always
meant to be that way.

whatever you decide
to do, I know it'll be
great.
because good lives in
you and it has a way of
seeping into everything
you do.

i was yours for a time
and for a time i thought
i knew it all.
who i was and the knowledge
of my purpose that came
with it.
i thought i knew where
i belonged and that's what
makes moving on so hard.
it's always hard to leave
home. even when you have
to accept it's not yours.

## WHERE TO FOLLOW JMSTORM

**FACEBOOK:** facebook.com/Jmstormquotes

**TUMBLR:** jmstormquotes.tumblr.com

**INSTAGRAM:** @jmstormquotes

**TWITTER:** @storm_jon

CPSIA information can be obtained
at www.ICGtesting.com
Printed in the USA
BVHW040505090920
588354BV00010B/520